Proceedings of a General Court-Martial upon Lieutenant Frederick Wood, of the Eleventh Light Dragoons

Anonymous

The Making of Modern Law collection of legal archives constitutes a genuine revolution in historical legal research because it opens up a wealth of rare and previously inaccessible sources in legal, constitutional, administrative, political, cultural, intellectual, and social history. This unique collection consists of three extensive archives that provide insight into more than 300 years of American and British history. These collections include:

Legal Treatises, 1800-1926: over 20,000 legal treatises provide a comprehensive collection in legal history, business and economics, politics and government.

Trials, 1600-1926: nearly 10,000 titles reveal the drama of famous, infamous, and obscure courtroom cases in America and the British Empire across three centuries.

Primary Sources, 1620-1926: includes reports, statutes and regulations in American history, including early state codes, municipal ordinances, constitutional conventions and compilations, and law dictionaries.

These archives provide a unique research tool for tracking the development of our modern legal system and how it has affected our culture, government, business – nearly every aspect of our everyday life. For the first time, these high-quality digital scans of original works are available via print-on-demand, making them readily accessible to libraries, students, independent scholars, and readers of all ages.

The BiblioLife Network

This project was made possible in part by the BiblioLife Network (BLN), a project aimed at addressing some of the huge challenges facing book preservationists around the world. The BLN includes libraries, library networks, archives, subject matter experts, online communities and library service providers. We believe every book ever published should be available as a high-quality print reproduction; printed on-demand anywhere in the world. This insures the ongoing accessibility of the content and helps generate sustainable revenue for the libraries and organizations that work to preserve these important materials.

The following book is in the "public domain" and represents an authentic reproduction of the text as printed by the original publisher. While we have attempted to accurately maintain the integrity of the original work, there are sometimes problems with the original work or the micro-film from which the books were digitized. This can result in minor errors in reproduction. Possible imperfections include missing and blurred pages, poor pictures, markings and other reproduction issues beyond our control. Because this work is culturally important, we have made it available as part of our commitment to protecting, preserving, and promoting the world's literature.

GUIDE TO FOLD-OUTS MAPS and OVERSIZED IMAGES

The book you are reading was digitized from microfilm captured over the past thirty to forty years. Years after the creation of the original microfilm, the book was converted to digital files and made available in an online database.

In an online database, page images do not need to conform to the size restrictions found in a printed book. When converting these images back into a printed bound book, the page sizes are standardized in ways that maintain the detail of the original. For large images, such as fold-out maps, the original page image is split into two or more pages

Guidelines used to determine how to split the page image follows:

• Some images are split vertically; large images require vertical and horizontal splits.
• For horizontal splits, the content is split left to right.
• For vertical splits, the content is split from top to bottom.
• For both vertical and horizontal splits, the image is processed from top left to bottom right.

PROCEEDINGS

OF A

General Court-Martial

UPON

LIEUTENANT FREDERIC WOOD,

OF THE

ELEVENTH LIGHT DRAGOONS

" Pour encourager les autres."

VOLTAIRE, UPON BYNG'S EXECUTION

LONDON

PRINTED FOR THOMAS BOONE, 480, STRAND.

1818.

Marchant, Printer, Ingram-court, London.

TO THE

OFFICERS

OF THE

ELEVENTH LIGHT DRAGOONS

THIS

PAMPHLET

IS INSCRIBED BY ONE,

WHO, DURING

Thirteen Years,

LIVED AMONGST THEM ON

TERMS OF UNBROKEN HARMONY,

AND WHO MUST EVER FEEL,

AS HE HAS THE

PRIDE AND PLEASURE TO SUBSCRIBE HIMSELF,

THEIR SINCERE FRIEND AND WELL-WISHER,

FREDERIC WOOD.

PREFACE.

THE following pages are at length reluctantly given to the army, for the sole purpose of correcting misrepresentation and error   Their publication has been delayed for a considerable period, but Mr Wood feels that he cannot longer withhold it, when so much falsehood is abroad, without compromising his own character and disappointing the just expectations of his friends.   He has deemed it expedient to publish his trial from notes transmitted to him through the office of the Judge-Advocate-General   It is true that these differ in many particulars from what his own recollection and that of his friends would have furnished, but he prefers adhering strictly to the official narrative, rather than to incur the charge of having moulded any part of the transaction to his own particular feelings

Enough, however, appears upon the face of this proceeding to establish a dismal anomaly in Military-Law   It must henceforth be taken as a precedent, that fifteen persons may meet together, *in Septc hir*, and upon their oaths decide the fate of a brother officer, "*after duly " and maturely weighing and considering the " evidence*" for and against him: and yet, *in the ensuing December*, that thirteen of these gentlemen may re-assemble, "*in pursuance*

" *of commands from His Royal Highness the*
" *Prince Regent,*" and without hearing any fresh
evidence, or again putting the prisoner on his
defence, annul and stultify their first opinion
and inflict a sentence the most severe within their
power

COURT MARTIAL.

PROCEEDINGS of a GENERAL COURT MARTIAL, held in the Second Division of Infantry, by virtue of a Warrant and in pursuance of an Order from Field-Marshal HIS GRACE the DUKE of WELLINGTON, K G and G C B Commander of the Forces, &c &c &c

Blendecques, 17th September, 1816

PRESIDENT,
Major-General Sir DENNIS PACK, K C.B

MEMBERS,

Lieut.-Colonel MACNEIL, 91st Regt

Major ROWAN, 52d

Captain PIDGEON, 71st

Captain MURPHY, 3d Foot.

Captain MACNEIL, 79th.

Lieut ROBERTSON, 79th

Lieutenant RHODES, 39th

Major HODGE, 29th Regt

Major REID, 71st

Captain GUN, 91st

Captain MACLEAN, 79th

Captain MACBEAN, 6th Foot

Lieutenant BOVILLE, 29th

Lieutenant GILDER, 6th

Lieutenant EDWARD BLAIR, 3d Foot,
Acting Deputy Judge Advocate

The Court having met pursuant to order, the Warrants, nominating and appointing the President, and also the Acting Deputy Judge Advocate, were respectively read in the usual form

Before the Court appeared, as Prisoner, Lieutenant FREDERICK WOOD, of the 11th Regiment of Light Dragoons, and acknowledged himself ready to take his Trial

The Court was sworn, and the Prisoner, Lieutenant Frederick Wood, arraigned on the following charges, viz

1st For unofficerlike and disrespectful conduct towards Lieutenant-Colonel Sleigh, his Commanding Officer, in having, on the evening of the 1st day of August, 1816, in the Mess-Room of the Regiment, and in the presence of other officers, replied to Lieutenant-Colonel Sleigh, who had said, in conversation respecting a regimental order, " That he, Lieutenant-Colonel Sleigh, was his " Commanding Officer there as well as in the Field," " That he, Lieutenant-Colonel Sleigh, was not," to the prejudice of good order and military discipline, at Wormhaut, in France

2d For unofficerlike and disorderly conduct and behaviour, at the Quarters of Lieutenant-Colonel Sleigh, his Commanding Officer, on the second day of August, 1816, in using reproachful and provoking speeches and gestures to him, Lieutenant-Colonel Sleigh, to the purport and effect following, and in reference to an order given by Lieutenant-Colonel Sleigh to Lieutenant Wood

" What breach of duty have I been guilty of,
" Sir, that I am to be superseded in my com-
" mand I will go and complain to the General,'
and on being desired by Lieutenant-Colonel
Sleigh to obey the order, and then to make his
complaint, saying, with great violence, " You
" had better not drive me to extremities, or I will
' blow your brains out! I am a gentleman's son,
" and your conduct is condemned by all the offi-
" cers, you have put up with insults from the
" subalterns, and had better retract, I will shoot
" you! you are a coward, and I will not be
" trampled upon, we both cannot live in the
" world," and, holding up his fist in a menacing
attitude against Lieutenant-Colonel Sleigh, repeating, with further violence, " You shall not live
" by G—d, if you drive me to extremities, I will
" shoot you! " to the prejudice of good order and
military discipline

3d For using reproachful and provoking language to
Lieutenant-Colonel Sleigh, tending to upbraid
him with having refused a challenge, and to excite
him to fight a duel with him, Lieutenant Wood,
to the effect following " Your conduct is con-
" demned by all the officers, you have put up
" with insults from subalterns, and by G—d, you
" had better retract, I will shoot you! you are a
" coward," at the time and place last mentioned

(Signed)   JOHN WATERS,
Lieutenant-Colonel and A A G

To which charges the Prisoner pleaded Not Guilty, and the Court proceeded to the examination of witnesses

LIEUT.-COLONEL JAMES WALLACE SLEIGH, commanding the 11th Regiment of Light Dragoons appeared as Prosecutor, who, being duly sworn, stated,

On the first of August last, I was dining at the mess of the 11th Dragoons, in the evening I heard a conversation at the bottom of the table, between Lieutenant Wood and another officer respecting the dress of the Regiment, when Lieutenant Wood asked Lieutenant Smith (I believe it was) to lend him the ornament of his chakos, to send to Paris, as a pattern, which I conceived very extraordinary, from the circumstance of orders having been given out for the officers to appear in them on the Sunday following, and I said, " do not take his, it is sufficient to have one without," when Lieutenant Wood replied, " I have been fifteen years in the service, " I know my duty perfectly, and in this room, I am " Mr Wood, and you are Mr Sleigh " I immediately told him, I was his commanding officer there, equally as in the field, and desired him to hold his tongue, and drop the conversation he replied, " *You are not*, and " if that is to be the case, I will not live at the mess; I " know my duty, and am allowed six months to wear my " clothes out, there has been an entire change in the " dress, and I will report it to the General " I again desired him to hold his tongue, which he did in a very disrespectful manner, snapping his fingers, and beating his hands, in a short time afterwards I left the room.

On the following morning, being the second of August last, after a field-day, I was writing letters in my room, when Lieutenant Wood came in very abruptly, and said, " What breach of duty have I been guilty of, Sir, ' that I am to be superseded in my command? I will " report it to the General." I answered, " Obey the orders " that have been given out, and then you may make your " complaint." Upon Lieutenant Wood becoming very violent, I went out of the room to call my servant, in order to send for the Adjutant, telling Lieutenant Wood, I would hear what he had to say, when the Adjutant arrived. On my sitting down in my chair again, Lieutenant Wood got into the most violent rage, saying, ' You had better not drive me to extremities, I am a " gentleman's son, your conduct has been condemned " by all the officers, you have been insulted by subal- " terns, which I can prove, and you had better retract, " or I will blow your brains out!'" I then said to him, " For God's sake be quiet for a moment only," when he repeated again, (getting into a greater rage if possible,) " I " will shoot you, you are a coward, we shall not both " live in this world together, I will not be trampled " upon, I will go and report you to the General, my " Commission is nothing." At this time he went to-wards the door, and I thought him going out of the room, but he returned again, doubling his fist, and sha-king it at me, saying, " You shall not live! you don't " know me, if you drive me to extremities, I will shoot

" you ' May I go to the General ?" I believe I replied, " You may," and he then left me in the same manner as he had entered the room

Question by the Court —To what command did the Prisoner allude, when he asked why he was superseded by your orders ?

A He had the command of a troop, and I removed him to another troop, which is, what I suppose, he alluded to

Q When was that order given

A. It was given *on the 2d of August* * I had arranged the removal some days previous

Q. *By the Prisoner* —Was the order for the ornaments given when I was with the regiment, or when I was absent ?

A. The order was given out, both at the time the Prisoner was with the regiment, and before he came to it Lieutenant Wood told me himself, he had seen the ornament with the Commanding Officer of the Depôt

Q At what time was the last order given ?

A I should think, about ten days before I heard the conversation at the mess, on the 1st of August

Q How long have I served with you in the 11th Dragoons ?

A I believe, about 12 or 13 years

Q What character have I borne, during that time, as an officer ?

---

* *Out of the usual course of orders* See Cornet Butcher's evidence, *Post* 14, and the Defence, *Post* 40—1

A I can say nothing against Lieutenant Wood's character, until this business, in his manner and conversation he is rather violent

Q Have I not been in the constant habit of commanding a troop?

A No except occasionally, when captains were absent

Q Have I never commanded a troop for two or three years at a time?

A *Never that I recollect* *

Q Was the troop taken from me on the second of August, and given to a senior or junior officer?

A To a junior Lieutenant

Q Did Lieutenant-Colonel Sleigh find any fault with my management of the troop, from which he last removed me, prior to this removal

A Yes, I have, the troop was going on very badly Lieutenant Wood shewed so great an unwillingness to improve himself in the drill of the regiment, that I conceived him to be an improper person to have the command of a young troop I must add, that this troop has been exceedingly improved since they have been under the charge of a junior officer

Q When did you so find fault

A Several times at Wormhaut, but I cannot state the exact days

---

* See the evidence of Captain Ridout, *Post* 45, and Captain Jenkins, *Post* 47

DANIEL LUTYENS, Esq

Paymaster of the 11th Dragoons, an evidence on the part of the prosecution, sworn and examined

Q *By the Prosecutor*—Were you at the mess of the 11th Dragoons on the first of August last?

A I was

Q. Did you hear the Prisoner, Lieut Wood, tell me, that in that room he was Mr Wood and I was only Mr Sleigh?

A Mr Wood did not state exactly those words, it was in consequence of the conversation that took place, that Mr Wood asked Colonel Sleigh, 'Are you speaking to me as the Commanding Officer to Lieutenant Wood, or as Mr Sleigh to Mr Wood?"

Q Did you hear Lieut Wood repeat, on my telling him I was his Commanding Officer, equally in that room as in the field, that I *was not*, and that, if that were to be the case he would not belong to the mess that he had been fifteen years in the service, and knew his duty perfectly?

A Mr Wood replied, "*very well, Sir,* I have been " fifteen years in the regiment, and have never been or- " dered by the Commanding Officer at the mess table " before to hold my tongue—if that is to be the case, I " will not live at the mess," and added, "I know my " duty to my Commanding Officer—I always have done " it, and will do it."

Q You have lived a long time at the mess of the 11th

Dragoons have you at any time heard any officer speak to me, or to any other officer in the command of the regiment in the way Lieut Wood did on that night, or behave so disrespectfully?

A I never recollect during the time I have been in the regiment, any similar circumstance, or such conversation occurring at the mess table

Q *By the Court* —Is the Court to understand that nothing passed which could bear the construction of disrespect, but what you have stated in your former answer?

A Mr Wood was remarkably warm, but I do not consider he meant to shew disrespect

Q Did you hear Lieut -Colonel Sleigh say, " I am your Commanding Officer here as in the field?"

A I did

Q What was Lieut. Wood's reply?

A As I have stated in my former answer

JAMES O'MEALLY, Esq

Surgeon of the 11th Light Dragoons, an evidence on the part of the prosecution, sworn and examined

Q *By the Prosecutor* —Were you at the mess of the 11th Dragoons on the first of August last

A I was

Q Did you hear Lieut Wood, in the course of the evening, tell me he was Mr Wood and I was only Mr Sleigh?

A *No, I did not,*—the question was asked, whether Mr Sleigh was speaking to him or Colonel Sleigh

Q Did you hear him repeat, on my telling him I was his Commanding Officer equally in that room as in the field, that *I was not,* and if that were to be the case, he could not belong to the mess,—that he had been fifteen years in the regiment, and knew his duty perfectly?

A On being told by Colonel Sleigh that he was speaking to him as Colonel Sleigh, his Commanding Officer, Lieut Wood said, that it was the first time in fifteen years he had been desired by the Commanding Officer to hold his tongue at a public mess room, and that he would not dine there any longer

Lieut WILLIAM SMITH,

of the 11th Dragoons, an evidence on the part of the prosecution, sworn and examined

Q *By the Prosecutor*—Were you at the mess of the 11th Dragoons on the first of August last?

A Yes; I was

Q Was not Lieut Wood asking you, or some other officer in conversation, to lend him an ornament for his chakos to send to Paris?

A Yes

Q Did you hear me say to Lieut. Wood, do not take another officer's, it is enough to have one without?

A Words to that effect

Q Did you hear him repeat, on my telling him, I was equally his Commanding Officer there as in the field, that *I was not,* that, if that were the case, he would not belong to the mess, that he had been fifteen years in the service, and knew his duty perfectly?

A I did not hear him dispute Colonel Sleigh's authority as Commanding Officer but I heard him say, that he had been fifteen years in the regiment, and that he knew his duty perfectly

LIEUT. CHARLES BACON,

of the 11th Dragoons, an evidence on the part of the prosecution, sworn and examined.

Q *By the Prosecutor*—Were you dining at the mess of the 11th Dragoons on the first of August

A Yes, I was

Q Did you hear Lieut Wood, upon my telling him I was his Commanding Officer equally there as in the field, say that I was not, that if that were the case he would not belong to the mess, that he had been fifteen years in the service, and knew his duty perfectly ?

A I did not hear him say that he, Colonel Sleigh, was not I heard Lieut Wood say that he should not dine here in future, that he had been fifteen years in the service, had always done his duty, and always would

LIEUT MILES SANDYS,

of the 11th Dragoons, an evidence on the part of the prosecution, sworn and examined

Q *By the Prosecutor*—Were you dining at the mess of the 11th Dragoons on the first of August last ?

A. I was

Q. Did you hear Lieut Wood, upon my telling him I was his Commanding Officer equally there as in the field, say that *I was not*, that, if that were to be the case, he would not belong to the mess, that he had been fifteen years in the service, and that he knew his duty perfectly?

A *I do not recollect Mr Wood having used the expression, Colonel Sleigh was not his Commanding Officer* —I heard Mr Wood say he had been sixteen years in the service I did not pay much attention, and do not recollect more of the subject

Cornet and Adjutant GEORGE BUTCHER, of the 11th Dragoons, an evidence on the part of the prosecution, sworn and examined

Q *By the Prosecutor* —Did Lieut Wood come to you after the field-day, on the morning of the second of August last, and inquire for me?

A Yes, he did

Q Did you observe any thing unusual or extraordinary in his manner?

A I was sitting in my office, with my back towards him when he came in, but I thought, by his manner of speaking, he was very much irritated

Q Did you not meet him going from my house, when I sent for you

A Yes, I did

Q What was his appearance at that time?

A. He was going very fast, and appeared in a great rage

Q Did I not tell you some days before Lieut Wood was removed from his troop, that I should be obliged to do so, from his inattention and dislike to learn his duty'

A Yes, you did, Sir

Q *By the Court* —How long before the second of August did Colonel Sleigh say he should be obliged to remove Lieut Wood?

A I cannot say positively,—it was between the 25th of July and second of August

It being now three o'clock, the Court adjourned, and at the particular request of the Prisoner, until Friday next, the twentieth instant, at eleven o'clock in the forenoon

---

SECOND DAY

Blendecques, 20th Sept 1816

THE Court having met pursuant to adjournment of the seventeenth instant, proceeded in the examination of witnesses

CORNET and ADJUTANT BUTCHER,

an evidence on the part of the prosecution, already sworn, again called and examined

By desire of the Court, his former evidence read over

Q *By the Court* —Was it previous to the evening of

the first of August, that Lieut.-Colonel Sleigh mentioned to you his intention of superseding Lieut. Wood in the command of the troop

A. Yes, it was

Q. Did he at the time distinctly state the reason for his doing so

A. He informed me, that the troop had not been taken that care of by Lieut. Wood that it ought to have been

Q. *By the Prisoner.*—What hour on the second of August last did the regiment return from the field?

A. I cannot say positively, but, to the best of my knowledge, it was between twelve and one

Q. State what hour the Colonel sent for you on the second of August last?

A. I should think about an hour after we came in from the field

Q. State at what hour, on the second of August last, you placed me under arrest?

A. To the best of my recollection, between four and five

Q. At what hour of the day was the order issued for my removal from the troop?

A. Immediately after the regiment coming in from the field day

Q. *Was that the usual hour of issuing orders?*

A. *No, it was not.*—It was a morning regimental order.

Q. State when you last delivered to the officers, the regimental cap ornaments

A. I gave one to Mr Sandys, on Friday last, and one I received at the same time for another officer

Lieut MILES SANDYS,

Of the 11th Dragoons, an evidence on the part of the prosecution, already sworn, again called and examined *at the desire of the Prosecutor*, his former evidence read over

Q *By the Prosecutor* — State the circumstances and conversation that passed, at the mess, on the first of August last?

A The first subject that Mr Wood introduced at the mess was about commissions, and afterwards the subject of cap-ornaments was introduced, which Colonel Sleigh had ordered every officer to appear in on the Sunday following. Lieut Wood said *they were foolish things*, and were near three pounds a set, adding, if any person would lend him a set, he would send to Paris and get a set that would do him equally well for a pound He continued talking in that way for some time, when Colonel Sleigh ordered him to provide himself with cap-orna-ments immediately, and said, that officers arriving from England ought to come out correctly dressed, or with proper appointments Lieut Wood answered, he had not seen the order, having been in England for a year After some further conversation Mr Wood said, *he thanked God that he had not Colonel Sleigh to thank for* *his leave of absence* Lieut Wood was then getting very warm, and he asked Colonel Sleigh if it was Mr. Wood and Mr Sleigh that were speaking Colonel Sleigh said no, he was speaking to Colonel Sleigh, the Commanding Officer, and as such he ordered him to hold his tongue Lieut Wood replied, that he had a right to talk at the mess he had been sixteen years in the service, *and was not to be frightened in that way,* he had done his duty, and would do it,—if Colonel Sleigh was Commanding Officer at the mess, he, Lieut. Wood, should not dine there I thought the conversation was then getting too serious, and I left the room in consequence, having never heard such conversation as that, on the part of Lieut Wood, take place at any mess before I further beg leave to add, *that Colonel Sleigh appeared to be perfectly calm,** during the time I was at the mess.

DANIEL LUTYENS, Esq

Paymaster of the 11th Dragoons, an evidence on the part of the prosecution, already sworn, again called and examined

By desire of the Court his former evidence was read over

Q *By the Court* —You have said, in your former evidence, that you never recollected any similar circumstance, or such conversation, at the mess before State

---

* See the evidence of Messrs Lutyens, Bacon, O'Meally, and Smith *Post*

now to the Court, what were the circumstances and conversation you alluded to ?

A As far as I can recollect it was about half past eight o'clock in the evening of the first of August, on a Thursday, Lieut Wood, in the course of conversation, was addressing himself to Lieut Bacon, who sat nearly opposite, requesting him to lend the ornament of his chakos, that he might be able to get one similarly embroidered for himself, as he was going to Dunkirk the next morning Colonel Sleigh here interposed, and said, that he hoped or wished Mr Bacon would do no such thing, as the person to whom he sent it would never return it—the consequence of which would be, there would be two officers without them, and it was quite enough to have one Mr Wood stated here, that it was not his fault he was then without the ornament,—that he had been absent nearly a twelvemonth with his family in Wales,— that, so situated, it was impossible for him to learn what changes had taken place in the dress of the regiment,— that on his joining the depôt at Romford, they were not worn by the officers there, and that he did not know, until he had joined the regiment in this country, that they were ordered to be generally worn by the officers. Colonel Sleigh afterwards remarked, that it only shewed Mr Wood had had too much leave, or too much indulgence Mr Wood then said, that he was not obliged to any body for the indulgence he had received, that he had been obliged to go home for the recovery of a wound, which he had received at the battle of Waterloo If it had been his wish to have prolonged his absence from the regiment he might have done so, as his wound was not perfectly healed when he joined the regiment. Colonel Sleigh after this said, that the ornament might be procured in the course of a few days from Mr. Hawkes, and that he expected to see Mr. Wood with it on the next Sunday's parade. Mr. Wood then addressed himself to Colonel Sleigh, putting the question stated in my former evidence,—" Am I to consider you speaking to " me as Colonel Sleigh to Lieut. Wood, or as Mr. " Sleigh speaking " to Mr. Wood ?" Upon which Colonel Sleigh answered, " I am speaking to you as Colonel Sleigh, " your Commanding Officer, and I order you to hold your " tongue." Mr. Wood continued—(what I have also stated in my former evidence) " Very well, Sir, I have been " thirteen years in the regiment, and have never been " told before, at the mess, by the Commanding Officer, " to hold my tongue. I know my duty to my Com- " manding Officer, I have always done my duty, and " always will do it." During this time Colonel Sleigh repeatedly said, while the conversation was going on, " Hold your tongue, Sir,"—" Hold your tongue, Sir." *Both parties* at this time were exceedingly warm, after which Mr. Wood became silent, and the conversation was not resumed.

Q. *By the Court* —How many officers were there present at that time ?

A. Five, besides the Prosecutor and Prisoner; there were also one or two strangers, not officers.

Q Did Mr. Wood say, he would not continue to dine at the mess, and if so, at what part of the conversation did he say so ?

A In that part of the conversation where Mr Wood says,—" Very well, Sir," he stated, if that were to be the case, (alluding to the order to hold his tongue) that he would not any longer live at the mess

Q *By the Prisoner* — Could any conversation have passed between the Prosecutor and Lieut Wood, at the mess, on the first of August last, without your hearing it?

A. No there could not

Q. Did you hear me say, that the ornaments were foolish things?

A. I do not recollect hearing any such thing

Q. You have stated, that I had no one to thank for my leave of absence; did I, at this time or any other, say, that I thanked God I had not Colonel Sleigh to thank?

A. No.

Q After what passed at the mess, did I ask you if you thought my conduct correct, and if so, what was your answer?

A The conversation was alluded to, after Colonel Sleigh left the room. Mr Wood mentioned his having been warm, but hoped he had said nothing that could be, as he expressed himself, " laid hold of."—I said it did not occur to me that he had.

Q. How long have you known me in the regiment, and state to the Court your opinion of my character as an officer and a gentleman?

A. I have known Mr. Wood twelve years, and I always have had every reason to entertain the highest opinion of his character, as an officer and a gentleman

Lieut CHARLES BACON,

of the 11th Dragoons, an evidence on the part of the prosecution, already sworn, again called and examined —By desire of the Court, his former evidence was again read.

Q *By the Court*—State to the Court, in reference to the first charge, the whole of the circumstances and conversation that occurred at the mess in the evening of the first of August

A The first I recollect was the mention of chakos ornaments and Mr Wood, as I conceived, addressing me, asked for the loan of a set, as he was going to Dunkirk, and would get them made by taking a pattern, as well as sending to England Colonel Sleigh, as I understood, remarked, I had better not, as they might fail to be returned, and it was sufficient to have one officer without them The next I recollect was, Mr. Wood saying he had been a long time in England, on joining the depot they were not worn there,—that he did not know of their being regimental Colonel Sleigh then said, *that* was the ill effect of officers having such long leave Mr Wood answered, he had been wounded at Waterloo, and in consequence had gone to England on sick leave—was therefore obliged to nobody for it. I cannot say whether he said he was not obliged to Colonel Sleigh, or whether he was obliged to nobody for it Colonel Sleigh here remarked, he did not wish to hear any more about it, and desired him to hold his tongue. Mr. Wood then asked, whether it was Colonel Sleigh addressing Lieut. Wood, or Mr Sleigh addressing Mr. Wood Colonel Sleigh answered, I am Colonel Sleigh, your Commanding Officer, and I desire you to hold your tongue There was some conversation passed afterwards, but I cannot speak to all of it. Mr Wood however said, he had been fifteen years in the service, that he had always done his duty, and always would

Q *By the Court* —Could any conversation have passed between Colonel Sleigh and Lieut Wood, on the above subject, without your hearing it

A I conceive there might, as I was in an inner room for a few minutes, and I cannot state what was the conversation at the time I left it

Q *By the Prisoner* —What is your opinion of my character as an officer and a gentleman, since you have known me ?

A As for Mr. Wood's character as an officer, I cannot, from my standing in the regiment, take upon me to say, but as to that of a gentleman, I have always found him completely so.

Q *By the Court* —Did Colonel Sleigh appear to be as warm as the Prisoner ?

A I cannot say ,—*both appeared to be warm*

JAMES O'MEALLY, Esq

surgeon of the 11th Dragoons, an evidence on the part of the prosecution, already sworn, again called and examined.

By desire of the Court his former evidence was read.

Q. *By the Court.*—State any farther circumstances or conversation, bearing upon the first charge?

A. I do not recollect any further circumstance than what is stated in my former evidence, unless I might be reminded of it by a pointed question.

Q. Were you present at the whole of the conversation between the Prosecutor and the Prisoner, on the evening of the first of August last?

A I was present the whole time.

Q. Could any conversation have taken place without your hearing it?

A. None,—but in a long conversation it is impossible to recollect all, where I was no way interested, and never expecting to be called upon the subject.

Q. Did you at any time in the evening hear the Prisoner say, that he thanked God he had not Colonel Sleigh to thank for his leave of absence?

A. I cannot say the exact words, but he certainly said, that he did not thank any one for his leave of absence—conceiving it to be sick leave, and more a leave of suffering than a leave of pleasure

Q. *By the Prisoner.*—State to the Court the appearance of my wound, on my rejoining the Regiment?

A. The wound was in the upper part of his leg, the integument adhering to the bone, and not perfectly, though very nearly, healed.

Q. Did you hear me in the course of conversation say, that the ornaments of the Regulation Caps were foolish?

A. I did not.

Q. **Was** Colonel Sleigh, throughout the whole of the conversation, perfectly calm?

A. *Both Colonel Sleigh and the Prisoner were warm*

Q. **Did** I, at the close of the conversation, ask your opinion of my conduct; and if so, what was your answer?

A. I recollect Lieutenant Wood's saying, after Colonel Sleigh left the room, that he hoped he had said nothing that was disrespectful, or nothing that could be taken hold of, and become the subject of a Court Martial. This was a question he asked generally, and I might have said, that I did not see or hear him say any thing that was disrespectful.

Q. What is your opinion of me, as an officer and a gentleman?

A. For the time I have been in the regiment, and known Lieutenant Wood, I have never heard, nor do I know, any thing that can tarnish his character in either respect.

Lieutenant WILLIAM SMITH,

of the 11th Dragoons, an evidence, on the part of the prosecution, already sworn, again called and examined. By desire of the Court, his former evidence was read.

Q. *By the Court.*—State any further circumstances or conversation, bearing on the first charge?

A. On the 1st of August, between 8 and 9 o'clock, at mess, the conversation turned upon the chakos ornaments; when Mr. Wood wished to borrow one, in order to send to Dunkirk, as he could get a person there to send the pattern to Paris, and have them made cheaper than in London, addressing himself more particularly to Mr Bacon. Colonel Sleigh remarked, I hope you will not lend them, as two officers will then be without instead of one. To which Mr Wood answered, it was not his fault, that he had been in Wales, they were not worn at the Depôt, nor did he know of any order for them to be worn, until he arrived in this country. On this, Colonel Sleigh replied, he had been too much indulged, and *that* was the consequence of officers having such long leave. Mr. Wood said, that he went home in consequence of his wounds, said he had suffered a great deal, and was not indebted to any one for his leave of absence, he could have had an extension, had he wished it, and that he had then joined before his wound was healed. The conversation went on, but I do not remember all of it, until Colonel Sleigh told Mr Wood to hold his tongue. Mr. Wood here asked Colonel Sleigh, if he spoke to him as Mr. Sleigh to Mr Wood, or Colonel Sleigh to Lieutenant Wood. Colonel Sleigh answered, I am the Commanding Officer here, and every where, and I desire you to get your regimental ornaments in four days. To which he replied, *I will*, that it was the first time he had ever been told by a Commanding Officer, at the Mess, to hold his tongue, and if that were to be the case, he would not dine there any more.

Q. *By the Prisoner.*—Did you hear me, in the course of this conversation, say, that the ornaments for the regimental caps were foolish things.

A. No.

Q. Did I say, that I was not indebted to any one for my leave, or that I thanked God, that I was not indebted to Colonel Sleigh for it?

A. Such as I have already stated, but I did not hear Colonel Sleigh's name mentioned at that time

Q Was Colonel Sleigh, throughout this discussion, perfectly calm?

A I should conceive not.

Q How long have you known me, and what is your opinion of my character, as an officer and a gentleman?

A I have known the Prisoner nine years, and always considered him a perfect gentleman, and a man of honour With respect to his character as an officer, being his junior, I shall only say, that I never heard any thing to his prejudice

Mrs SARAH RUTLAND,

an evidence on the part of the prosecution, sworn and examined

Q. *By the Prosecutor* —Did you see Lieutenant Wood on the 2d of August, when he came to my house?

A I did.

Q What did he say to you?

A He asked me if Colonel Sleigh was at home, and I answered, yes he then asked me if the Colonel was alone, to which I also replied, yes.

Q Did you hear any thing particular after he went up stairs?

A I heard Mr Wood in a great passion, and I think

he made use of the word, " Coward," but I am not positive

Q Did you see Mr. Wood when he left the house? And was there any difference in his manner from what there is in general?

A I saw, by his countenance, he was in a great passion.

Q. Did Lieutenant Wood usually ask you if I was alone, when he came to my house?

A. I never recollect his doing so before.

Q. *By the Court.*—Where were you when you overheard what passed?

A I was standing at the back door

Q. Where was the Colonel's room?

A It was over the back door, and both windows were open.

Q. How long do you think Mr. Wood remained in the room, where Colonel Sleigh was?

A About twenty minutes, or a quarter of an hour. I am not positive, it might be more or less.

Q. *By the Prisoner.*—Have you never said, that you knew nothing at all about this transaction?

A. *I have.*

Q. How long have you been in the service of Lieutenant-Colonel Sleigh?

A. Nearly five years.

Q. Do you usually answer visitors? And is it customary for subalterns, waiting upon the Colonel, to ask if he his alone?

A I frequently answer visitors; but I do not know whether it is usual to ask if the Colonel is alone.

Here, it being three o'clock, the Court adjourned until to-morrow, the 21st instant, at ten o'clock in the morning

---

THIRD DAY.

Blendeques, 21st September, 1816.

The Court having met pursuant to its adjournment of yesterday, continued on the examination of witnesses.

LIEUTENANT MILES SANDYS,

of the 11th Dragoons, an evidence on the part of the prosecution, already sworn, recalled by the Court.

Q *By the Court*—Referring to your former evidence, on the first day's sitting, in which you say, you did not pay much attention to, or recollect more of the subject, how came it, on your second day's evidence, that all the circumstances therein stated, reverted so cleanly to your mind?

A. On the first day, I gave direct answers to the questions asked me, conceiving it to be my duty not to animadvert upon the subject, but, on the second day I was called before the Court, I was desired to state every thing I knew that passed on the occasion, which I did to the best of my knowledge

Q. Were the notes, to which you found it necessary to refer on your second day's examination, with you during the first day's evidence?

A *I believe* they were not *

Q Had you any conversation with the Prosecutor, since your first examination, on the subject of the trial?

A I had I stated to Lieutenant-Colonel Sleigh what passed at the Mess.

Q. How was the conversation brought about?

A I was over at Head-Quarters the day after the Court Martial sat, and I met Colonel Sleigh, after putting up my horse, *who asked me to go into his house with him In the course of our conversation,†* he asked me to state to him the conversation that occurred at the mess, which I accordingly did

Q You have stated, in your first evidence, that you paid little attention to what passed What was the cause of your taking notes respecting that conversation? And when were they made?

A In the former part of my evidence, wherein I gave

---

* The Judge-Advocate's report (to an exact copy of which this is confined, for reasons given in the Preface) sadly curtails this gentleman's explanation

† *The whole* of this conversation (*interesting* no doubt to a degree) the Court would not allow to be given —The lieutenant's answer to the last question is *extremely* lucid and intelligible

my answer, respecting the latter part of the first charge, saying, " Lieutenant Wood had been sixteen years in the " service, was not to be frightened in that way, and " Colonel Sleigh ordered him to hold his tongue I said, " I paid little attention to what passed," meaning, that I left the Mess immediately after the conclusion of that sentence

The notes were made a day or two before the first assembly of the Court Martial They were voluntary, and from my own recollection, not suggested by any one, but framed for my own protection, conceiving I was to be cross-examined by the Prisoner's Council

Here the Prosecutor stated, that he had no further evidence to call on the charges before the Court

DEFENCE.

The Prisoner, being put upon his defence, addressed the Court as follows

Mr. President, and Gentlemen of this honourable Court,

THE evidence on the part of the prosecution being at length closed, I beg permission to address to you some observations in my own defence, and, in the exercise of this privilege, I shall purposely abstain from framing any laboured appeal to the indulgence of the Court, because I feel *that* to be a boon, which the courtesy of gentlemen and brother officers would be certain to yield to me in *every* place, and under almost *any* circumstances, and I am therefore most confident that it will not be withholden in a place like the present,—set apart for the high purposes of justice; and under circumstances so serious to the individual accused, involving upon his part every thing that is dear to him as a man, an officer, and a gentleman.

With this impression, Sir, I feel that it would indeed be superfluous to solicit for my case, that which I am sure the Court are predisposed to bestow upon it,—a fair and a patient consideration.

Sir, at the close of a service which has honourably employed fifteen of the best years of my life, and after hav-

ing passed through that period without reproach or re-
buke of any kind, I find myself to day unexpectedly
called upon to confront, in a Court, my Commanding
Officer, who seeks to take from me, *upon his single unsupported* testimony, that rank and character which it
has cost so large a portion of my days to attain and
establish.

Sir, I esteem myself most fortunate that in this moment of hazard and difficulty, I have been brought before
gentlemen, whose honour, feeling, and discrimination,
place them beyond the reach of prejudice of any kind —
And I have even now to thank them for indulgence
and kindness, which suffice to banish from my mind
every apprehension as to the result of their deliberations.
Sir, I am thus without alarm, because I know and feel
myself to be without guilt I am fearless, because I am
innocent,—and the experience of all my life has taught
me, that however ably malice may perform its work,
TRUTH *must in the end prevail*

Sir, the charges which have been preferred against
me are three in number, but I think it must be obvious
to the Court, where the strength of the prosecutor's case
is intended to rest. He seems to have been aware that
his purpose would have been endangered, by the mere
production of himself in the *double* character of prosecutor and witness. He felt doubtless, that before a tribu-
nal such as this, the unassisted deposition of one individual against another, (whilst that other was precluded
from the right of replying upon oath) would be received,
to say the least, with the extreme of jealousy and caution.

—His own prudence could not fail to suggest, that, in such a case, men of sense and feeling would weigh well and often the exceeding bias and interest which must belong to such a prosecutor, and impel him to convict *by any means* the party he accuses. Under this impression, he has (fortunately for me) ventured to prefer *one* charge which my brother officers might have attested, and by which the Court will be enabled to estimate the credit due to his single unconfirmed recollections, and upon this charge I put it to the Court, with the extreme of respect, but also of confidence, whether he has not entirely failed.—I ask them on their honour to declare, whether the witnesses produced by himself (five in number) have in any respect borne out his accusation? Colonel Sleigh has indeed, as was to be expected, told his own tale with considerable dexterity, he has garbled a conversation which took place at a dining table, in the hour of open unsuspecting confidence, and which Mr O'Meally has truly told you he little expected would become the subject of investigation like this, and, by selecting some expressions in it which did really occur, and adding others which did not, he has endeavoured to bring home to me a charge of disrespect—and how has he succeeded? The Court will have the goodness to bear always in their minds, that the charge which we are now discussing is confined within the narrow limits of a single expression. It imputes to me simply, that when the Colonel asserted he was my Commanding Officer at the mess as well as in the field, I replied " he was not." And what, I would ask, do the witnesses say as to the conversation out of which this

charge arises?—now that the Court have kindly antici-
pated my wishes and defence, and drawn forth from them
the WHOLE of it. The first of these who is called (Mr
Lutyens) an officer of considerable character and standing in the service, states, that my answer to the Colonel's assertion of his rank being equal at the mess as in
the field, was in these terms, " *Very well, Sir,*" (a
term surely rather affirming than denying the fact) and
that I went on to state (which after a command so un-
gracious as that which Mr Lutyens tells you Colonel
Sleigh so often repeated, " *Hold your tongue,*" I trust
the Court will not consider intemperate), " that I had
been fifteen years in the service, and had never before
been ordered by my Commanding Officer at the mess
table to hold my tongue,—that if that were to be the
case, I would not live at the mess,—*That I knew my
duty to my Commanding Officer, that I always had done
it and always would*"

Sir, upon the last sentence of this reply, I would take
leave to observe, in passing, how improbable, to say the
least, it renders the charge we are now discussing, which
supposes, that I *began* this reply with a flat negation of
the prosecutor's authority, for, if correct, it imputes to
me the singular inconsistency of denying, in one sentence
of a remark, that authority which I take pride to myself
for having always observed, and always resolving to observe, in the next. The next witness, Sir, Mr O'Meally
deposes to my reply to the Colonel, in nearly the
same terms as Mr Lutyens, making it commence with the
assertion, " of my having been 15 years at the mess."

Mr Smith contradicts Colonel Sleigh's assertion, that
I addressed *him in particular* on the subject of the ornament, and is express to the point, that I did not dispute

the Colonel's authority as my Commanding Officer; and Mr. Bacon deposes to the same effect, and even Mr. Sandys, who concluded his very short testimony, on Tuesday last, by saying, that he did *not pay much attention to the conversation, and did not recollect more of the subject,* (for which words I beg to refer the Court to their minutes) and *yet,* when called upon yesterday, could detail, at greater length than any other, the *whole* of what passed, and put into my mouth expressions which escaped the ears of Mr Lutyens, Mr O'Meally, Mr. Smith, and Mr Bacon, who are *all* agreed in denying that I used them — Even this gentleman, I say, refreshed as his memory has been within two days, did not, and does not *even yet* recollect that I uttered the words, upon which alone the first charge is grounded. *Where* then, I repeat, is the testimony to convict me on this part of the accusation

Thus, Sir, do we find, in the very outset of this extraordinary case, the Prosecutor, on whose single unsupported testimony, as to the second and third charges, my rank and character are placed in hazard, MIS-STATING FACTS, confuted by all to whom he appeals, and unable to set up, even from the unguarded language of a messtable, the *shadow* of an accusation

But, Sir, I cannot dismiss altogether the first of these charges, without adverting very briefly to some of those extraneous topics into which Colonel Sleigh, in giving his testimony, thought fit to wander I entreat the Court never to forget, that it was he who first began to digress from the point immediately in issue before them, and I beg to assure the Court, that I have neither wish nor intention to follow him, further than is needful to correct mis-statement and error. He began his evidence by speaking of a conversation that took place on the subject of a regimental ornament, and now that the whole of this conversation is before you, it remains with yourselves to determine (foreign as it is to the charge) who commenced, and who chiefly was to blame throughout the transaction to which it refers. Sir, upon the subject of this ornament, I call to mind the expression of the Court, on Tuesday, " that it was wholly irrelevant to the charge ," and, in humble acquiesence with their opinion, I forbear to offer to you all the testimony, with which I might have furnished myself, to establish the impossibility of my being at the moment provided with it. The Adjutant has told you that, even so late as the moment when the Court was sitting upon Tuesday last, he was distributing these ornaments to some of the officers, and the fact is, that for that purpose he received on that day two of them from myself, which had arrived, together with my own, from London. Upon this subject, therefore, I will only add, that upon the Colonel's own statement, I could not be in any wise culpable, in as much as the order given out, (he admits,) did not direct them to be worn till the Sunday ensuing the day of this discussion, and, of course, *till that period arrived,* no possible breach of obedience could be incurred.

Sir, the Colonel has also introduced into his testimony on the first charge, an observation on my manner and gestures, as being disrespectful towards him. Upon this subject, however, you have the evidence of Mr. Lutyens, (the Prosecutor's own witness) who states to you, " that although my manner was warm, he did *not* consider " that I meant to shew disrespect," and Mr. O'Meally deposes, that to a question from myself, involving the same fact, he gave at the time, and when all the circumstances were fresh in his memory, a decided negative, and upon this subject, I would call to the remembrance of the Court, with the utmost humility, that, at the moment when my passions are supposed to have gained so completely the ascendant over my reason and temper, it is in proof that I was yet so able to restrain and bring them under controul, that when Colonel Sleigh, in the course of the discussion, ordered me, in no very gracious or gentle tone, to provide myself with the ornament within four days, I replied to him, in terms of plain unequivocal submission, " I will," or " very well," or words to a similar effect   After this, will it be contended, that I had disrespect, either in my manner or my mind? Sir, Mr Lutyens has told you, that I was warm, and (in this, as in every other particular) he has spoken nothing but the truth   But the cause of this warmth, which had been artfully concealed by the Prosecutor, is now laid before you, and I hope the Court will observe how much this disclosure varies the state of the case   Colonel Sleigh led you to believe, that, at once, and in a moment, and without provocation of any kind, (save that which might arise out of the mention of the ornament so often alluded to) I became outrageous and violent   But, Sir, the evidence now upon your minutes will furnish, I humbly submit, a weightier ground for my indignation   It was, not that the Colonel rudely interfered in a conversation wholly addressed to another, and desired Mr Bacon *not* to comply with a request which had no motive but the fulfilment of his orders —It was, not that he repeatedly told me to hold my tongue,—but it was, Sir, I confess, that he threw out, in the presence of the assembled mess, a plain insinuation, that I had prolonged unfairly the absence allowed to me, in consequence of my wound at

Waterloo, in other words, that I had skulked, in England, away from my duty and my regiment This, Sir, I protest to you, upon my honour, as a man and a soldier, was the single cause which created warmth, (if there wa any) either in my manner or method of expression, and a warmth, Sir, *it will always be remembered,* of which Colonel Sleigh partook in an equal degree with myself Sir, if this unprovoked allusion be established, (and upon the evidence it cannot be denied) I put it to the Court, who are men of feeling as well as honour, **to** make some allowance for an officer attacked upon so tender a point, and **I** throw myself for an apology upon every feeling that belongs to the nature and the profession which is common to us both

But, Sir, I will detain you no longer upon the first of these accusations, in which the evidence of one individual (*who is the Prosecutor and party most anxious to convict me*) is opposed to that of *five* disinterested persons, free from even a suspicion of prejudice, and I hasten to consider the second and third charges preferred against me Sir, I think I may begin, by asserting these to rest *altogether* upon the testimony of Colonel Sleigh, for, with regard to the deposition of the Adjutant, it establishes only that, when I passed him in my way from the Colonel, my step was hasty, and my manner, *as he thought,* irritated, a fact certainly of very little import in a criminal proceeding of this moment, and which (even if Cornet Butcher's opinion be correct as to mere personal appearance, and he does not state that *I said* any thing) might have arisen from causes very distinct from an altercation with my Colonel. The Colonel has indeed, as a last resource, produced one other person in support of this case, *whose name did not even appear in the list given in with the charges to the Court and myself.* Sir, I can assure you most unfeignedly, that I approach the testimony of this unfortunate woman, with all possible reluctance and pain, and as I feel that her evidence is of little if any importance, I had rather avoid if possible, bringing my brother officers into so painful and delicate a situation, as that of compelling them to state their opinion of the relation in which she stands to the Prosecutor But, Sir, to what does her testimony amount She confesses on my first question to her, that she has often told persons, (and two of these persons I can produce,) *that she knew nothing at all about the transaction*, and upon her evidence, she states herself not to be *positive,* as to even hearing the solitary word which she has mentioned, and surely, Sir, a person who has professed *entire ignorance,* and is even now full only of *recollections* and belief, and especially, Sir, a person such as Mrs Rutland, is not to be attended to in a prosecution like the present She said that I asked if the Colonel was alone, a mark of respect, without which, I believe, few subalterns would intrude into the presence of their superior, and as to my being in anger, I have no hesitation in avowing, that I was indeed far from composed, being, at the moment to which she speaks, on my way to the General, to complain of my removal from my troop I repeat, Sir, that when the testimony of the Adjutant and herself are considered, it weighs not a feather in the scale, and leaves the Prosecutor to support the case upon his own unassisted oath.

And here then, unfortunately for me, the testimony of my brother officers, which has thus long served to refute the assertions of the prosecutor, forsakes me, and from the nature and necessity of the case, I am left to meet my opponent single-handed, without the power of disproving any thing that he chooses to advance; and whilst *he* is permitted to verify his statement by the solemn sanction of an oath, I am, on the other hand, confined to simple protestations of my innocence In a situation of such infinite moment and difficulty to the party accused, it will not, I trust, be thought too much to entreat the Court (in forming their conclusions) to consider *well and often*, the very suspicious circumstances under which this *prosecuting witness* appears before them They will doubtless remember, that he is a witness already, on the evidence produced by himself to the first charge, *contradicted*, and that he has proved himself capable of imputing to me an expression that had no existence but in his own imagination, and the fair and obvious inference from this, I submit to be, that if he thus could transgress the line and boundary of truth, when others were present to disprove and correct him, much more will he be likely to do so, when without check or controul, and free from the *possibility* of detection

Sir, if no charge had indeed preceded the one in question, and if nothing but Colonel Sleigh's testimony appeared in the case, the very great improbability of an officer being base enough to fabricate a tale like this, might, and must, have occurred to every one But, Sir, I submit, that the prosecutor has already proved by his former testimony, how small are his scruples, and has forfeited, by the matter and manner of that evidence, all claim to the credit, which (in other circumstances) the feeling to which I have alluded might, perhaps, procure for him

Sir, I must entreat, also, the Court to consider in my behalf, the improbabilities of the story which he tells An officer of fifteen years standing in the service, and having, in age, long passed that period when the passions run away with the reason, conceives himself aggrieved by his Commanding Officer, and goes to him (as military etiquette prescribes) to solicit leave to complain to his General. And this purpose, *the Court will please to recollect*, Colonel Sleigh himself admits, that I carried into effect, for he makes me ask permission at the close of the supposed conversation, " to go to the " General," and states that " *he believes he gave it*," but by *his account*, BEFORE I preferred this request, I poured out upon him a torrent of abuse, outraging all discipline and decorum. AND THEN, after having forfeited (if his account be true) my commission twenty times over, *then, and not till then*, I asked his permission to go to the General. For what purpose, Sir, could I then want the General? Was it to tell him how I had been using my Commanding Officer? Was it to be dragged from his presence (as I must have expected to be) into immediate arrest? Surely, had I resolved upon so rash and desperate a step as that imputed to me, the house of the General was the last place to which I should have bent my steps. To have gone thither at such a moment, would have been worse than nugatory and useless; it would have been the extreme of folly.

But the Colonel states, that he *did* give me leave, which is one of the facts to which he has truly deposed, and I shall prove to you that I acted upon that leave—that I saw the General, and preferred my complaint, and that I then returned to Colonel Sleigh, and made him acquainted with the nature of my interview with the General, that I then quitted him WITHOUT MOLESTATION, and that it was not until four hours had elapsed that I was put into arrest, as appears by the evidence of the Adjutant Butcher,—*for what crime*, until Sunday last, but from report, I knew not

Sir, if I had indeed, treated Colonel Sleigh as he describes, is it probable that he would have *allowed* me *first* to go to the General, then to return to camp, and then to be at large a considerable time, without taking *any* notice of so flagrant an outrage? Sir, the plain and obvious course for him to take was to call at once his Adjutant, (who states himself to have been close to the Colonel's quarters,) and place me in immediate arrest, but, no! he occupies a space of *four hours* in meditating upon that, which, *if true*, could require no meditation at all, and *then*, having doubtless planned the scheme of my destruction, takes *at length* the first step towards its fulfilment

Sir, in a proceeding like this, where every thing depends upon the testimony of one solitary witness, it is of great importance to bring home to the breast of that witness a malicious feeling towards the person he accuses, and for that purpose I beg leave to advert to the order issued by Colonel Sleigh to remove me from the troop, of which, previous to this dispute, I had the command, and placing me under *the only senior subaltern* in the corps, and which, with the permission of the Court, I will read to them in its exact terms

Wormhaut, August 2, 1816

" Lieut Wood is transferred to C Troop, and will
" join it to-morrow, at Houndscotte the officer com-
' manding *will* report his arrival, *and is responsible for his*
" *not leaving it, until he has fully complied with* **the**
" **orders relating to officers' dress.**"—(those orders, which
last Tuesday only were not obeyed by the majority of

the officers)—" Lieut Rotton will take the command of
" Major Horsley's troop

" By order, &c &c "

Sir, I think that the feeling and motive which called
forth this document is, upon the face of it, most appa-
rent If Colonel Sleigh had, indeed, as he has stated
to you, resolved for more than a fortnight upon my removal from the troop, in consequence of my unfitness to
command it, it is singular, not only that he should wait
fifteen days, whilst the troop by his own account was going to ruin, before he took a step so essential to the good
of the service , but also, that the order announcing his
intention should have appeared on the day *immediately
succeeding that on which the conversation at the mess occurred* , and it is *more singular*, that it should have appeared,
not in the regular course of regimental orders (in which
case it would have been issued and promulged on the
evening of the day *after* the mess conversation*)* but *as
an after order* (as has been proved to you by Mr Butcher)
coming forth on the spur of the moment, in the interval
between the breaking up of the mess and the close of
the field-day in the morning, which is precisely that interval when Colonel's Sleigh's passions against me must be supposed to have been most inflamed And, Sir, it is *above all
extraordinary*, that this order should allude (as it does in
express and unusual terms) to the regimental ornament
which had been so much discussed on the evening before; and should, moreover, forbid my leaving my quarters, until provided with that which, so late as Tuesday last,
you have heard that many of the officers were without

Sir, I hope I may be allowed to add, as an addi-
tional improbability attending upon this charge, my cha-

racter and the length of my services in the army. As to the former of these, the Court will remember that I fearlessly put to my prosecutor a question directly involving it, and that he replied, that until the present instance, he knew nothing against me. And I have also put, and shall continue to put, to the officers who have appeared, and will appear before you, with an equal absence of apprehension, a similar interrogatory. Colonel Sleigh did, indeed add a remark on the warmth of my temper, and I have no wish to conceal from the Court, that nature has implanted in me much that is quick and susceptible, but in making this avowal, Sir, it is some satisfaction for me to reflect, that this quickness of feeling has never once, during fifteen years broken in upon the friendship and good humour in which I have hitherto lived with my brother officers.

To the length of my services as a subaltern, I have had frequent occasion to recur in the course of this address, and I will only add, that during this protracted period, I have suffered both in the prisons and from the sword of the enemy. Sir, I must repeat that it is little probable, that an individual who has toiled thus long in a profession, and bestowed upon it so large a portion of his time, and means, and constitution, should at once, and in a moment by conduct so flagrant as that which is imputed to me, render useless the labour of years, and for ever shut the door upon advancement and hope.

Sir, I have already stated, that upon a charge of this description, resting only upon the testimony of one witness, it is out of my power to produce to the Court direct exculpatory proof, and I will therefore bring to a conclusion this lengthened address by an entreaty which I would press by every thing most solemn upon the attention and conscience of the Court I would adjure them to consider again and again, before they pronounce a verdict, (which is to entail upon me consequences so afflicting,) what a serious (and I may say unusual) thing it is to convict upon the bare unsupported oath of an individual, who is both prosecutor and witness, and beyond the reach of all possible contradiction The law of our country has prescribed a rule, binding upon *all* Courts, military as well as civil, *that no person shall be permitted to give evidence in his own cause* And will any one who has heard this proceeding, assert that *this is not* the cause of Colonel Sleigh —his cause emphatically, and to the letter,—begun, continued, and ended as it is, upon his single unsupported testimony

Gentlemen, I repeat to you, (and it is my concluding remark,) that whatever be the result of your deliberations, it will be received by me with the extreme of deference and respect, but, as it concerns myself, with comparative indifference If I fall, I shall fall, as thousands have done before me, the victim of perjury and malice, but I shall carry with me into my retirement a feeling, of which Colonel Sleigh has no power to deprive me, and compared with which, every calamity must appear insignificant,—a feeling of conscious innocence!

With these observations, adding only to them my thanks for the manner in which they have been received, I proceed to call my witnesses

WITNESSES FOR THE PRISONER,

LIEUT-COLONEL RICHARD DIGGINS,

of the 11th Dragoons, an Evidence on the part of the defence, sworn and examined.

Q *By the Prisoner*—How long have you known me in the 11th Dragoons, and state to the Court your opinion of my character, as an officer and a gentleman?

A. I have known Mr. Wood ever since he belonged to the regiment. It has been many years, however, since he was under my command; as I have been absent from the regiment these six years past, and have only rejoined within the last six months. But while Mr Wood was under my command, I ever found him an attentive good officer; and, in every instance his character perfectly that of a gentleman.

CAPTAIN GEORGE RIDOUT,

of the 11th Dragoons, an Evidence on the part of the defence, sworn and examined.

Q *By the Prisoner*—How long have you known me, and state to the Court your opinion of my character, as an officer and a gentleman?

A I have known Mr Wood ever since he has been in the regiment, thirteen years, and have always considered him an honourable, an upright, and a perfect gentleman

Q Did I ever command your troop, during your absence? and if so, state to the Court what was the condition of the troop on your return?

A I was absent from the regiment, during the years 1809, 1810, and the spring of 1811 On my return, the regiment being ordered on service, I found Mr Wood in the command of my troop, and on going to the then Commanding Officer of the regiment, Colonel Cummins, I remember his saying to me, " You ought to be very " much obliged to Mr Wood, he has done ample justice " to your troop in your absence I consider it now to " be one of the finest troops, if not the finest, in the re- " giment, and it is owing to his exertions, it having " been one of the junior troops " I certainly considered Mr Wood as an active zealous officer.

Captain THOMAS BINNY,

of the 11th Dragoons, an Evidence on the part of the defence, sworn and examined

Q *By the Prisoner* —How long have you known me, and state to the Court your opinion of me, as an officer and a gentleman?

A I have known Mr. Wood about eight years, and have always had the highest opinion of his character, both as an officer and a gentleman.

Captain JOHN JENKINS,

of the 11th Dragoons, an Evidence on the part of the defence sworn and examined

Q *By the Prisoner*—How long have you known me, and state to the Court your opinion of my character, as an officer and a gentleman?

A I have known Mr Wood near ten years, have always found him to be a man of honour, considered him a good soldier, and particularly a good troop officer

Cornet WILLIAM JORDAN,

of the 11th Dragoons, an Evidence on the part of the defence, sworn and examined

Q *By the Prisoner*—How long have you been in the regiment?

A Twenty-two years, and upwards

Q. Did you march with me, when I had the command of a squadron, from Romford to Woimbaut, and if so, what attention did I pay to it?

A In my opinion, Mr Wood paid every attention, and wished to bring the squadron in good order to the regiment

Here the Prisoner stated, that he closed his defence.

REPLY *

The Prosecutor addressed the Court, in reply, to the following effect —

The Prisoner having finished his defence, I beg permission to offer a few words, before the Court proceed to their final decision

Of all the duties a Commanding Officer is called upon to perform, that of prosecuting an officer is assuredly the most painful and embarrassing

For the first time in my life, that office has now fallen to my lot, and I will hope, that I have endeavoured to proceed with the least aggravation to the charges compatible with my duty, in substantiating them by the best evidence, of which they were susceptible I do assure the Court, that my bringing them forward has not arisen from any pique or personal ill-will towards Lieutenant Wood, with whom I have lived, and until very lately thought I did, on intimate and friendly terms

With respect to the first charge, on the prosecution of which, some of the evidence have stated my temper to

---

* This *supposed* reply *might* have been *handed in* by the Prosecutor to the Judge Advocate, but certainly was *not* delivered Every officer present must be aware, that Colonel Sleigh merely stammered out a few sentences, and then—sat down The history of the transaction, I dare to say, is this—The Judge Advocate (a sensible gentlemanly man) wrote the reply, but the Colonel was unable to deliver it However, it is here given as what was *meant* to have been said !

be warm, I only appeal to any Commanding Officer of a regiment, who is anxious for the credit of his corps, and who had issued orders, nearly six months previous, for the officers to complete themselves in their dress, what he would have thought, in hearing an officer, only three days before *that* fixed on which every one was to appear uniform, say, that he had not completed himself, and was then only beginning to think of it

Lieut Wood joined the regiment in June --He knew his name had not been sent to the Adjutant, like others, in order to be forwarded to London, to obtain the necessary ornaments He must have seen several in the caps of the officers present with the regiment, and therefore should have exerted himself in procuring them

I expected on seeing an officer join from England, after twelve months absence, that he would have been complete in every thing, but instead of this, Lieut Wood appeared without any part of his dress except his jacket Two months I waited with patience to see the orders complied with—they were not The same negligence appeared on the part of Lieut Wood towards his troop; I heard endless complaints, I found repeated fault with it I likewise proved Lieut Wood could not put his men through the requisite exercise, and by his manner, and in his conversation, it was easily perceptible how much he was averse to learn what was necessary to perfect him in his duty

From unforeseen circumstances, Lieut Wood has not been more than ten months present with the regiment during the last six years After such a period of retirement from active service, let an officer's standing be what it may, he must obviously require much of both attention and practice to recover a competent knowledge of his profession I therefore trust the Court will feel I have not acted with severity in removing Lieut Wood from the command of a young troop that demanded the most watchful and unremitting attention

With regard to the charges before the Court, I had, as a Commanding Officer of a regiment, no alternative,—nothing was left to me but to lay the conduct of Lieut Wood before my superior officer, and in the two last, I did not trust to my memory *I committed to paper all that he had said, the moment he had left my room,** his endeavouring, in the latter case, to invalidate the testimony of my only witness (a *respectable* person), by an assertion void of truth, and an insinuation of the most mischievous tendency, although couched in the smoothest and most artful terms, is an attempt that I trust the Court will not pay attention to for a moment Indeed, he will have appeared only to offer an accession of strength to this very evidence, if any it had needed, by hazarding assertions which he has not even attempted to establish.

His strong and pointed remarks touching my not having placed him in immediate arrest are easily and obviously accounted for I did not do so, that he might have a fair opportunity of seeing Major-General Sir Colquhoun Grant, and that he might not with justice say thereafter, I had prevented his complaining against me

---

* A gentlemanly mode of proceeding ! ! !

Indeed, had I pursued a different course, I might well have been charged with warmth of temper, but granting as I did the free exercise of that privilege, which is the right of every officer to complain where he thinks himself wronged, and reflecting in the mean time that Lieut Wood's conduct had arrived at that pitch which the strong arm of authority alone could restrain, I hesitated no longer to perform a duty, however irksome, nor delayed reporting it to my superiors

With respect to the latter part of the defence, wherein an allusion is made to the possibility of his fall by means of malice and of perjury —weak in argument, although strong in language, it carries with it its best and surest refutation It is a position untenable as it is unsolid, taken up, as it should seem, solely for the purpose of being abandoned,—the expiring effort of a bad cause, and the advancement of an opinion, serving only to shew the impossibility of its proof

I have now only to thank Sir Denis Pack, and the Members of the Court, for the time they have allowed me to detain them, and I beg to repeat that the course I have pursued has arisen from any thing but pique or personal ill will It has been imposed on me as an imperative duty, undertaken solely for the good of his Majesty's service, and performed, as I am bound, to the best of my ability, in the situation I hold as Commanding Officer of the regiment

The Court adjourned until Tuesday next, the 24th instant, at eleven o'clock in the forenoon

Blendecques, Sept 24th, 1816

OPINION

THE Court having deliberately and maturely weighed and considered the evidence adduced in support of the prosecution, together with what the Prisoner hath said and offered in his defence, is of opinion, with respect to the first charge, viz —For unofficerlike and disrespectful conduct towards Lieut.-Colonel Sleigh, his Commanding Officer, in having on the evening of the first day of August, 1816, in the mess-room of the regiment, and in the presence of other Officers replied to Lieut.-Colonel Sleigh, who had said in conversation respecting a regimental order,—" That he, Lieut. Colonel Sleigh, was " his Commanding Officer there as well as in the field, " that Lieut. Colonel Sleigh was not," to the prejudice of good order and military discipline, at Wormhaut, in France,

That the Prisoner is NOT GUILTY of the said first charge, the precise words alleged as constituting the offence having not been proved, and the Court doth therefore acquit him thereof

With respect to the second charge, viz For unofficerlike and disorderly conduct and behaviour, at the quarters of Lieut.-Colonel Sleigh, his Commanding Officer, on the second day of August, 1816, in using reproachful and provoking speeches and gestures to him, Lieut.-Colonel Sleigh, to the purport *and effect* following, and in reference to an order given by Lieut.-Colonel Sleigh to Lieut Wood " What breach of duty have I been " guilty of, Sir, that I am to be superseded in my command, I will go and complain to the General " And on being desired by Lieut Colonel Sleigh to obey the order, and then to make his complaint, saying with great violence, " You had better not drive me to extremities, " or I will blow your brains out I am a gentleman's son, " and your conduct is censured by all the officers You " have put up with insults from the subalterns, and had " better retract—I will shoot you You are a coward, " and I will not be trampled upon, we both cannot live " in this world —And holding up his fist in a menacing attitude against Lieut-Colonel Sleigh, repeating with further violence,—" You shall not live by God,—if you " drive me to extremities, I will shoot you'—To the prejudice of good order and military discipline,

The Court is of opinion, that the Prisoner is GENE-RALLY GUILTY, but not to the full extent affirmed in the said second charge, the words alleged not having been clearly made out

With respect to the third charge, viz —For using reproachful and provoking language to Lieut-Colonel Sleigh, tending to upbraid him with having refused a challenge, and to excite him to fight a duel with him, Lieut Wood, to the effect following —" Your conduct " is condemned by all the officers You have put up " with insults from subalterns, and by God you had bet- " ter retract,—I will shoot you you are a coward "— At the time and place last-mentioned,

The Court is of opinion, that this charge has not been

proved against the Prisoner, and doth therefore AC-QUIT him of the said third charge

The Court having found the Prisoner, generally, GUILTY upon the second charge, as recited in their opinion above set forth, and which being in breach of the articles of war, the Court doth adjudge him, the Prisoner, Lieut Frederick Wood, of the 11th Regiment of Light Dragoons, to lose his rank in that regiment, so far as shall place him next and immediately under Lieut James Richard Rotton, of the same corps, and further to be publicly and severely reprimanded, at such time as his Royal Highness the Prince Regent, in the name and on the behalf of his Majesty, may be pleased to direct.

D PACK,
Major General and President

EDW BLAIR,
Lieut 3d Foot,
Actg. Dep Jud Adv

Lilliers, 2d Dec 1816
Memorandum

The above recited opinion and sentence was cancelled this second day of December, 1816, as recorded on the accompanying revised decision

D PACK,
Major General and President

EDW BLAIR,
Lieut 3d Foot,
Actg Dep. Jud. Adv

REVISION

Lieut WOOD, 11th Dragoons

Lilliers, Nov 9th 1816

The Court, with the exception of some members unavoidably absent, re-asembled this day in pursuance of the commands of his Royal Highness the Prince Regent, as communicated by H R H the Commander in Chief, (through his Grace the Duke of Wellington,) bearing date, " Horse Guards 25th of October, 1816, for the " purpose expressed therein, of revising their finding on " the separate charges, in order to clear up the ambi- " guity at present resting upon it."

And *the commands* of his Royal Highness the Prince Regent having been duly read and communicated, the Court thought fit thereupon immediately to pro eed to a reconsideration of the whole of the proceedings on the case before them, discussing the various points at issue, with a *reference to the instructions* * afforded in the communication above alluded to, and continuing in close deliberation until three o'clock, at which hour the Court coming to no decision, (being under thirteen in number,) adjourned until such future day as should hereafter be named by the President

---

* What those instructions were, we have never been able to ascertain Their *purport*, however, may be guessed

REVISION

LIEUT WOOD, Second Day

Lilliers Nov 22, 1816

The Court, with the exception of *some members still absent*, re-assembled this day, in pursuance of its adjournment of the 9th of November instant, and in obedience to division orders, bearing date " Nauvinyham, 19th Nov 1816

But the number of the members present being under that prescribed by the Mutiny Act, and Articles of War, the Court again adjourned, until such further day as should afterwards be named by the President

REVISION

LIEUT WOOD, Third Day

Lilliers, Dec 2, 1816

The Court re-assembled this day, in pursuance of its adjournment of the 22d Nov ult and in obedience to division orders, dated " Lilliers, 30th Nov 1816 '

The Court recommenced its deliberation on the whole of the subject matter at issue, on the charges against the Prisoner, Lieut Frederick Wood, and, after a mature discussion of all the points to be examined, *with a due consideration to the instructions* conveyed in the commands of His Royal Highness the Prince Regent*, have there-

---

* What instructions   What commands   The second sentence tells us, if the Judge Advocate will not

upon *cancelled,* and do hereby cancel and rescind their former finding and sentence, declaring the same to be void and of no effect, equally as if such finding and sentence had never been recorded ; and the Court doth now pronounce the following decision, as their revised and final judgment on the aforesaid several charges

OPINION.

The Court having deliberately and maturely weighed and considered the evidence adduced on the part of the prosecution, against the Prisoner, Lieut Frederic Wood, of the 11th Regiment of Light Drrgoons, together with what he hath said and offered in his defence,—is of opinion that he is *guilty* of the several charges exhibited against him, to the prejudice of good order and military discipline, and in breach of the articles of war Whereupon the Court doth sentence and adjudge him, the Prisoner, Lieut. Frederic Wood, of the 11th Regiment of Light Dragoons, TO BE CASHIERED.

D PACK,
Major General and President

EDW. BLAIR,
   Lieut 3d Foot,
Actg Dep Jud. Adv

(A true Copy.)

J A. OLDHAM

Judge Advocate General's Office,
13th January, 1818.

Extract of a Letter, from HIS ROYAL HIGHNESS the DUKE of YORK, to HIS GRACE the DUKE of WELLINGTON

" *I am to acquaint your Grace, that His Royal High-*
" *ness was pleased, in the name, and on the behalf of His*
" *Majesty, to approve and confirm the finding and sentence*
" *of the Court. But taking into consideration all the cir-*
" *cumstances attending the evidence, and particularly the*
" *previous good character of Lieutenant Wood, His Royal*
" *Highness was pleased to command, that the sentence should*
" *be mitigated by his being placed upon half pay* "

THE END.

Lightning Source UK Ltd.
Milton Keynes UK
UKHW031149020322
399454UK00007B/1281